The Water Cycle

Written by Alison Milford

Contents

Exploring the water cycle	2	Drinking water	26
Precipitation	4	How we use water	30
Surface run-off	6	Human effects on	
Water underground	8	the water cycle	32
Evaporation	12	Climate change	36
Transpiration	14	Extreme weather	38
Condensation	16	The water footprint	40
Clouds	18	Don't waste water!	42
Where does it rain?	20	Glossary	44
Forecasting rain	22	Index	45
How nature needs water	24	Water world	46

Collins

Exploring the water cycle

What should we drink to keep healthy? What do plants need to help them grow? The answer is water.

You may think that drops of water are newly made but, in fact, water is being renewed over and over again in a natural recycling process called the water cycle.

There are parts of the water cycle that we can see, such as clouds, rain and sun, but there are also other important parts that we can't see. This book explores how the water cycle works and how water affects our lives and the future of our planet.

> **Did you know?**
> Millions of years ago, dinosaurs drank the same water we use today!

The water cycle

sun

clouds

condensation

precipitation

transpiration

run-off

evaporation

Precipitation

Rainfall

The water cycle is like a cycle wheel, with no exact start or end. Perhaps the best place to start is when water rains down from the sky. This is called precipitation.

Precipitation happens when water droplets in the clouds become too heavy to carry and have to fall to the ground.

Did you know?
Rain drops fall in flat oval shapes and can be different sizes.

1 mm   2 mm   3 mm

rain drop shapes

Some larger raindrops form shapes like this.

Snowfall

When the air is very cold, the water droplets freeze and fall as snow instead of rain. Snow can fall during winter and all year round in places with cold **climates** such as the Arctic and Antarctica.

Sleet is a mix of rain and melting snow.

Hailstones are hard balls of frozen water droplets.

Surface run-off

Water run-off

When you tip a bucket of water down a slope, the water flows down to the bottom. Water always flows downhill. As a result, water flows downhill in streams and rivers or collects at the bottom of hills in lakes.

This part of the water cycle is called the run-off. The water runs off the land into lakes, or streams and rivers, which flow into an ocean or sea.

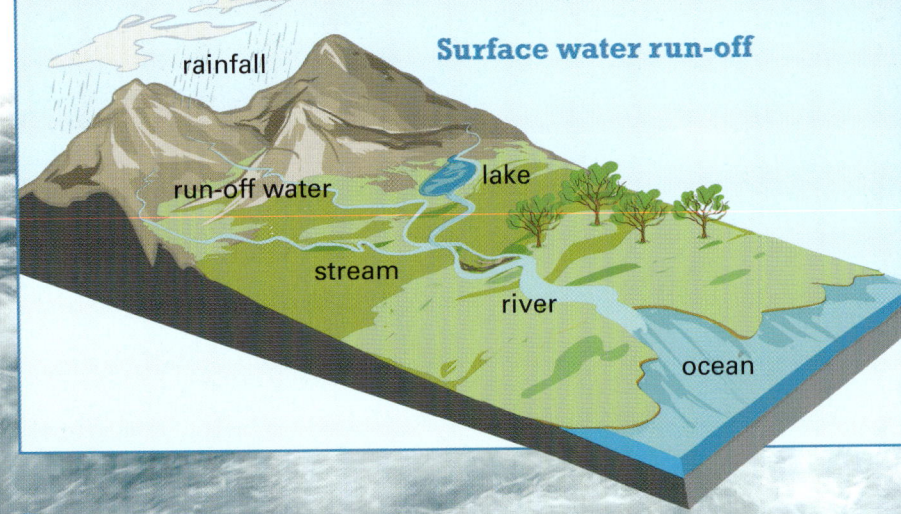

Snow run-off

During springtime, warm air melts the snow that's fallen in cold places such as mountain tops. The melted water, called meltwater, flows quickly down streams and rivers to join other run-off water.

Did you know?
Lots of meltwater and run-off water can cause major floods.

Water underground

Ground water

Water is everywhere – even under our feet! As rainwater runs off across the land some of it seeps through the soil into the ground below.

Collecting ground water experiment

This experiment shows how groundwater collects.

- Put a kitchen towel over a cup.
- Slowly pour water over the towel.
- Some water stays on the towel.
- Some water seeps into the cup.

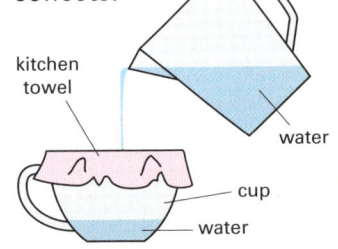

Rivers and lakes can also be found underground.

Some ground water joins underground channels flowing into rivers and oceans above ground.

Aquifers

Most of the world's **fresh water** is stored underground. This happens when ground water finds its way into small open areas between rocks. These storage areas are called aquifers.

This well has been dug to get fresh water from an aquifer.

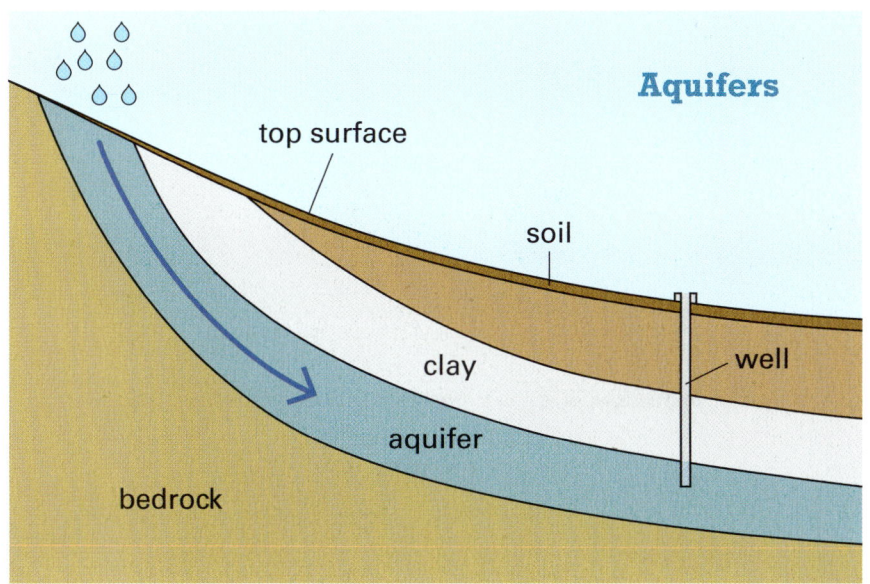

Surface water drains

In a rainstorm, water can fall on to the roads. However, thanks to square holes at the side of the road, they rarely flood. These holes are called surface water drains.

The grating stops rubbish getting into the drain.

The rainwater runs towards the kerb and through the drain into an underground pipe.

The rainwater then flows along the underground pipe until it comes out into a large water outlet such as a river, **canal** or sea.

These people are exploring underground drain-water pipes. It would be dangerous to go down there just after a rainfall as the pipes would be filled with rushing water.

Evaporation

After a rainfall, most surfaces are wet with water but, after a while, it disappears. So where's it gone?

The answer lies with the sun. Its heat turns the water into a **vapour** or gas. This water vapour then rises back up into the sky on the warm air. This is called evaporation.

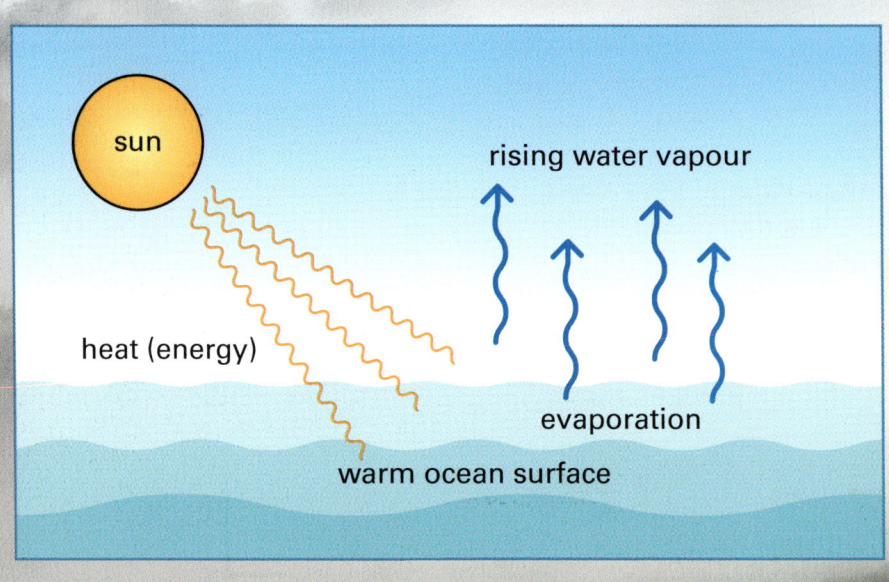

Speed of evaporation

Water evaporates at different speeds.

Try this evaporation test:

- Soak two pieces of cloth with water.
- Put one in a cool place.
- Put the other in a warm place.

Which cloth's water evaporates first?

Answer: The cloth in the warm place. The warm air helped evaporate the water quickly.

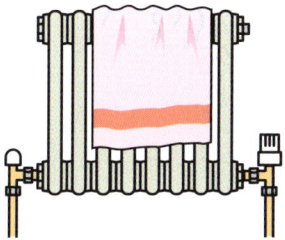

Did you know?
Water vapour can travel thousands of kilometres in the air.

Transpiration

Most plants need water to grow. They also play an important part in the water cycle.

When it's warm, humans sweat and plants transpire.

1 Ground water or run-off water

2 Water travels through the roots and stem, into the leaves.

3 Tiny holes allow the plant to breathe out invisible water droplets.

4 The droplets evaporate back up into the air.

This process is called transpiration.

Transpiring plants

If you place a clear plastic bag over the top of a plant and put it somewhere warm, you'll soon see that the bag has water droplets on it. These are the water droplets that the plant is transpiring or breathing out.

Did you know?

On a hot day, a tree can transpire over 1,300 litres of water into the air. That's enough to fill this tank!

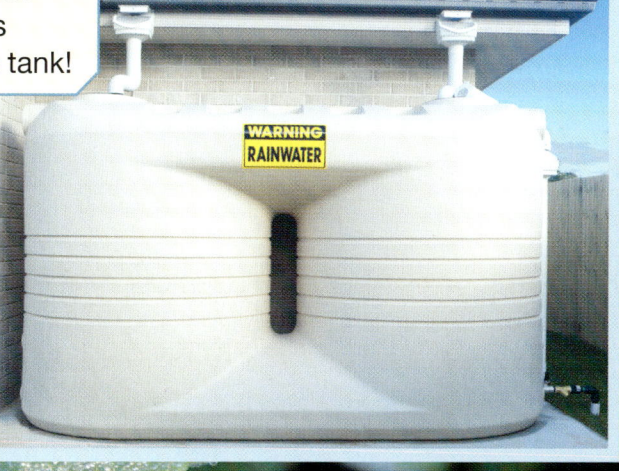

Condensation

When it's cold outside and warm inside, water droplets can appear on the inside of windows. This is because the evaporated water in the warm air turns back into water droplets when it hits the cold window.

In the water cycle, the higher the water vapour rises, the colder the air gets. Eventually the cold air turns the vapour back into water. This change is called condensation.

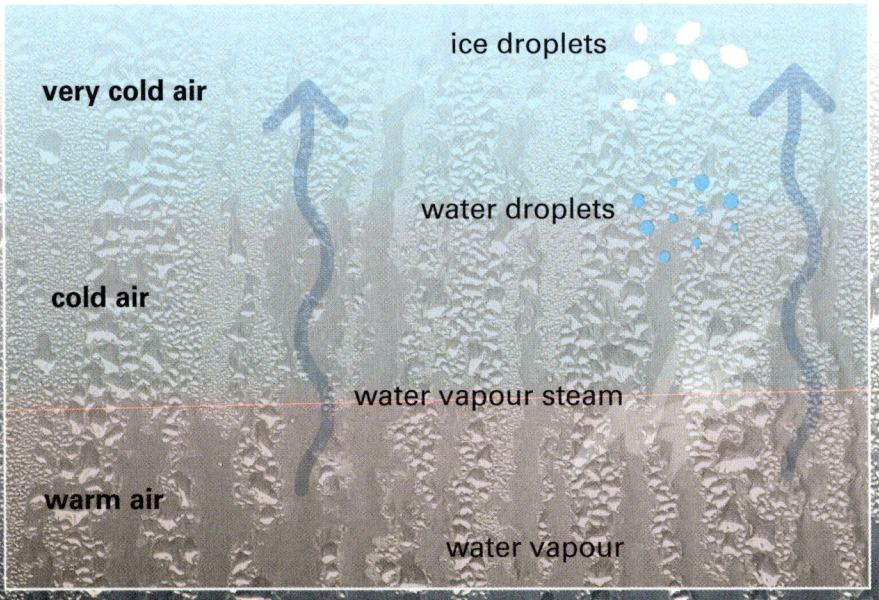

Dew

Early in the morning, droplets of water can appear on grass and thin objects such as cobwebs. This is called dew.

Dew happens when warm vapour from the soil rises during the night and touches something cooler. As a result, the vapour condenses into dew drops.

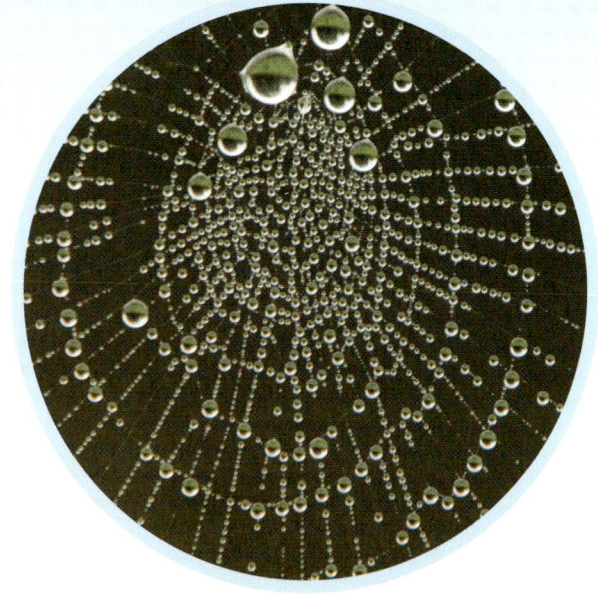

Frost is frozen dew.

Clouds

Clouds are actually millions of tiny condensed water droplets joined together. As they cross the sky, clouds get bigger and heavier until the water droplets fall back down to Earth again. Once the water has gone, the cloud disappears – and so the water cycle goes round again.

Thick rain clouds look dark because they're full of rain drops. This stops the light shining through them.

Heavy rain is falling from this rain cloud.

Cloud spotting

Use this cloud spotter to help you find them in the sky.

cirrus		• thin, wispy and white • move quickly in wind
alto		• cover the sky • grey and blue colour
strato		• cover the sky • greyish colours
cumulus		• white and puffy • flat base and towering top

Where does it rain?

Some places have a high rainfall. This is partly because they're near large areas of water, such as oceans, rivers and lakes, where more water vapour condenses into rain clouds.

Very dry places, such as the desert, don't have as much rain as there's not a lot of water that can rise up and condense into clouds.

The wet monsoon

During their hot summers, India gets very heavy rain storms called the wet monsoon.

Warm air filled with water droplets is blown inland from the Indian Ocean by the monsoon winds. When the heavy rain clouds are blown into the cool mountains of India, they burst (like water balloons bursting when they hit something) and drop a lot of rainwater.

Forecasting rain

People have always tried to predict when it would rain. In the past, they would often look at clouds or signs in nature to see if rain was on its way.

Today, weather forecasters called meteorologists use charts, computers and other devices to help them predict when and where it'll rain.

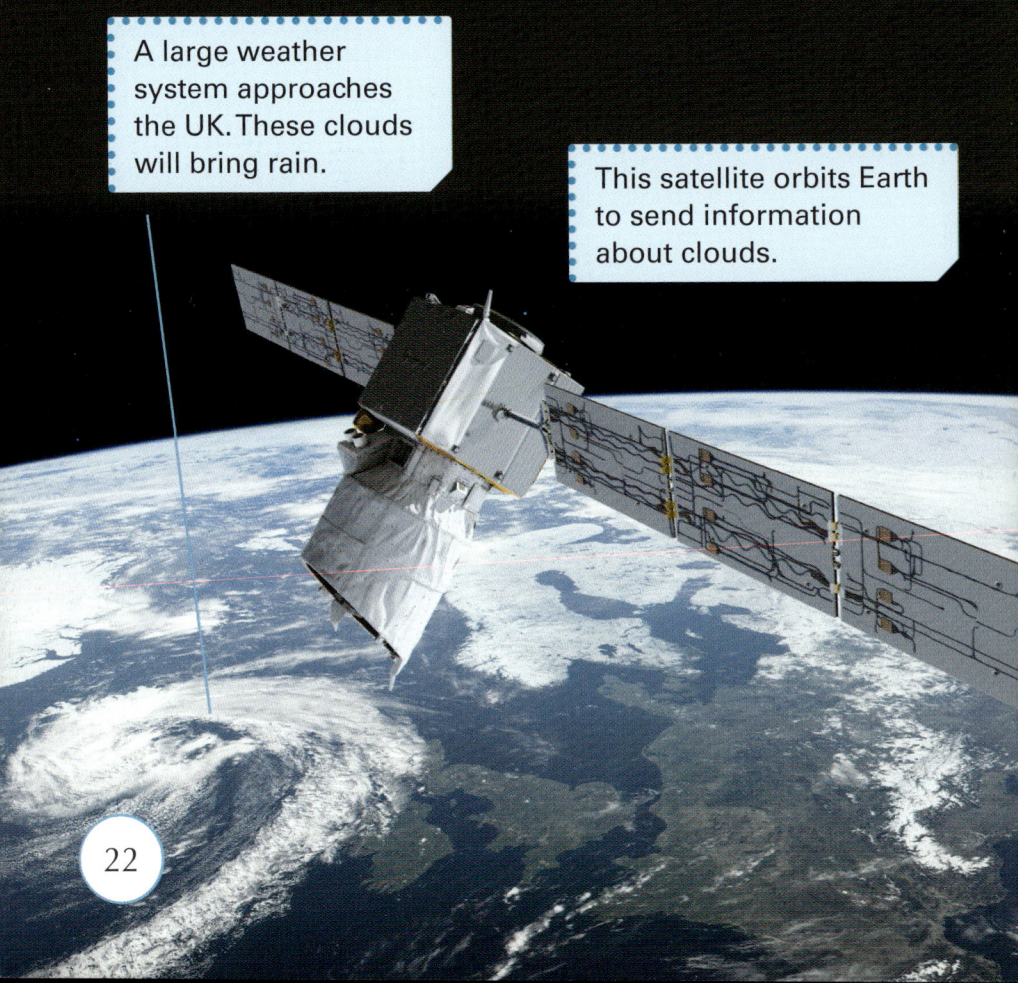

A large weather system approaches the UK. These clouds will bring rain.

This satellite orbits Earth to send information about clouds.

Doppler radar

Forecasters also use radars to find out about the weather. A weather radar uses radio waves to find out where rain is likely to fall and how heavy it will be. This is what a radar reading looks like.

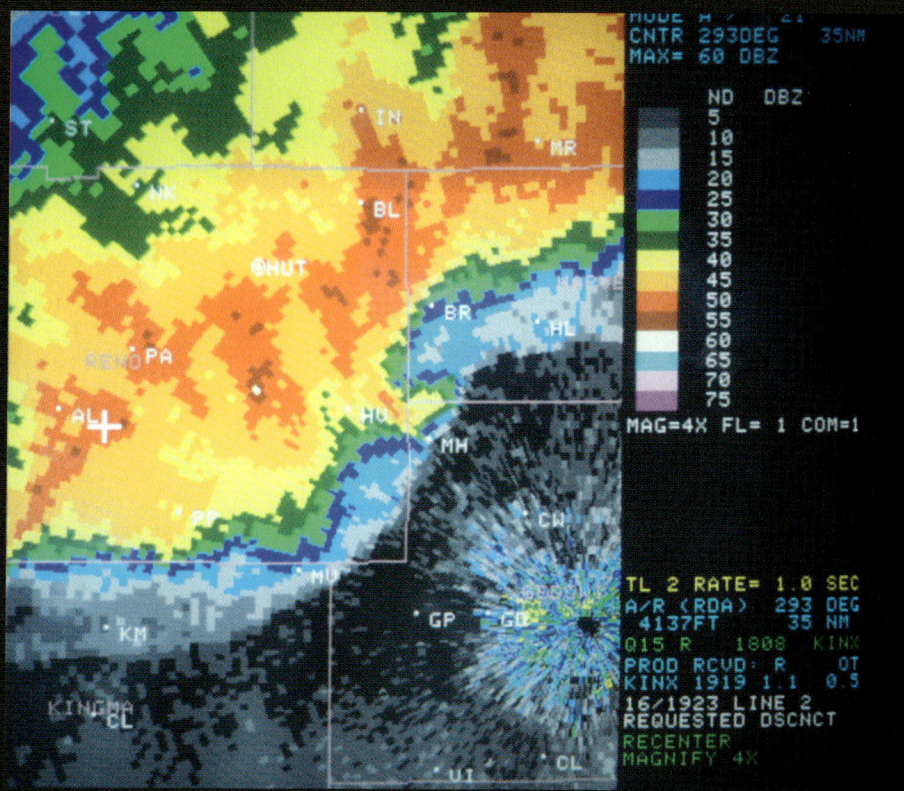

This shows how much water could be in a rainstorm. The areas in red will have the heaviest rainfall.

23

How nature needs water

The rainforests are a very important part of the water cycle.

Rainforests are forests of tall trees with smaller plants beneath them. They grow in a hot climate with lots of rain. There are rainforests in Central and South America, Australia, Asia and parts of Africa. The world's largest rainforest is the Amazon Rainforest in South America.

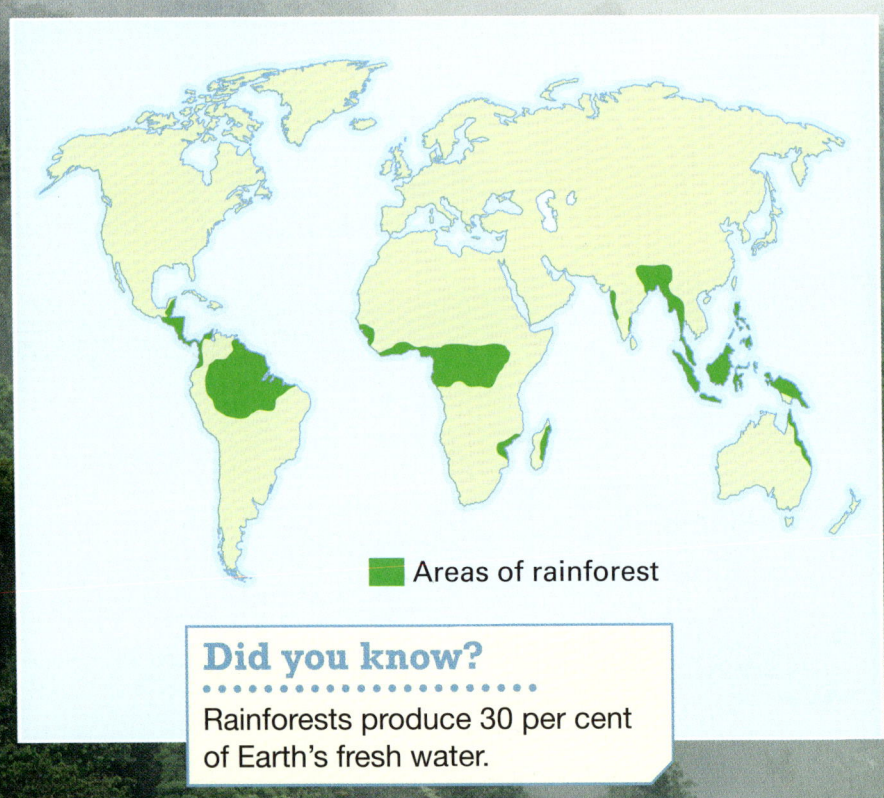

Areas of rainforest

Did you know?
Rainforests produce 30 per cent of Earth's fresh water.

A rainforest water cycle

Rainforests transpire lots of water vapour into the air. As the air heats up, it can feel heavy with water. This is called humidity.

As well as helping Earth's water cycle, the rainforest also has its own water cycle. Half of its rain is recycled from its own evaporated water.

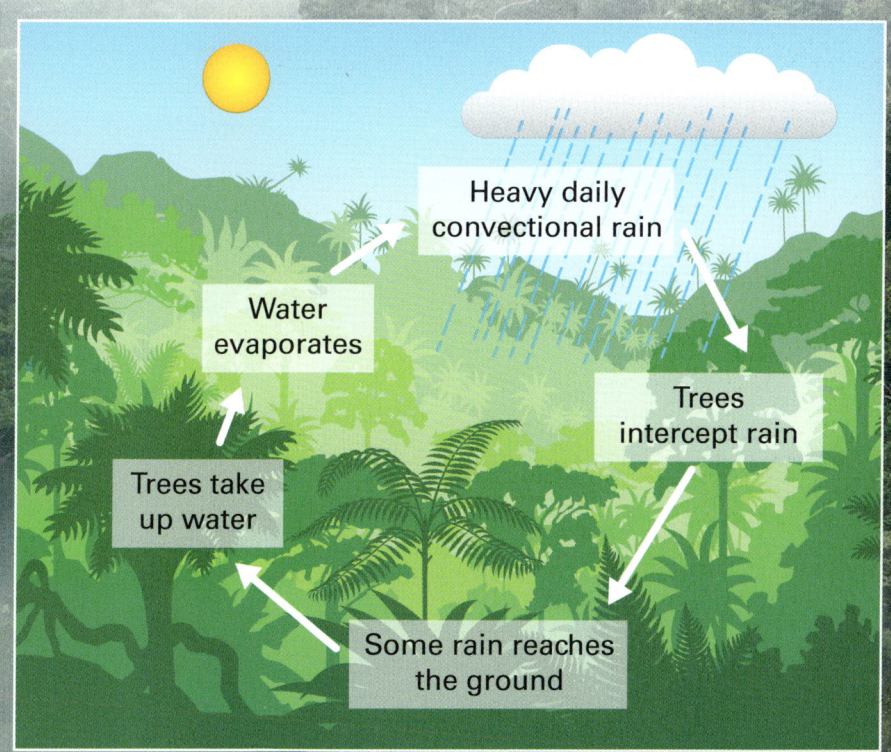

Drinking water

To get a drink of water, we can just turn on the tap. However, our drinking water has to go through a lot of changes before it gets there.

Follow the flow chart to find out how.

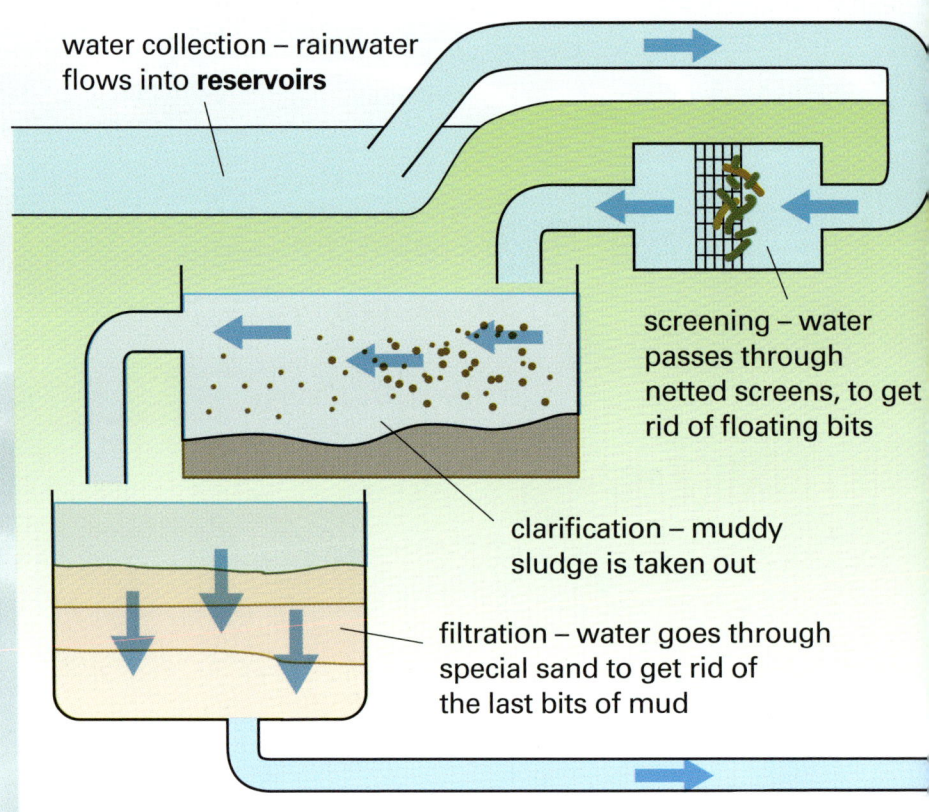

water collection – rainwater flows into **reservoirs**

screening – water passes through netted screens, to get rid of floating bits

clarification – muddy sludge is taken out

filtration – water goes through special sand to get rid of the last bits of mud

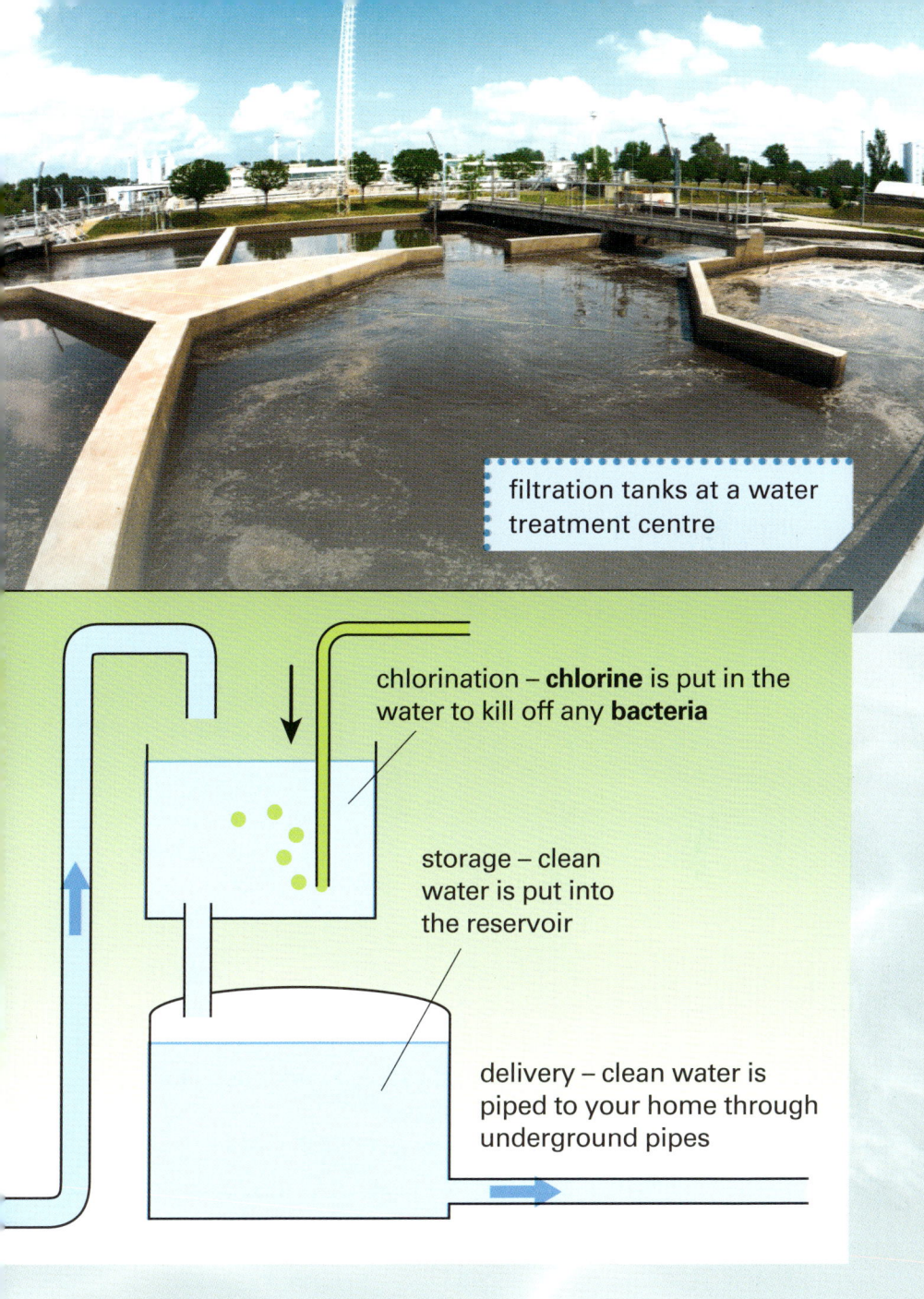

filtration tanks at a water treatment centre

chlorination – **chlorine** is put in the water to kill off any **bacteria**

storage – clean water is put into the reservoir

delivery – clean water is piped to your home through underground pipes

Clean drinking water

Not everyone's lucky enough to have clean, safe drinking water. In some countries in Africa, Asia and South America, many people become ill or die from drinking water that contains harmful bacteria.

Did you know?
About 750 million people don't have clean drinking water.

The dirty water may make this child ill.

Water projects and inventions are helping thousands of people to get clean drinking water.

Some villages and towns use new strongly-built wells to bring up fresh, clean water from underground aquifers.

women and children collecting drinking water from a manmade well

This is a filter bottle. The dirty water is pumped through a filter to get rid of dirt and bacteria. The water is then clean to drink.

How we use water

Water plays a very important part in our lives and it's used for lots of different things.

Everyday use

We use water every day for things such as drinking, washing clothes and ourselves, flushing toilets, cleaning and cooking food.

Fun activities

We use water and ice for fun activities and sports such as swimming, water parks, ice-skating, rowing and skiing.

Growing fruit and vegetables

Water is used to help our fruit and vegetables grow.

Fire safety

Water is used by firefighters to stop fires.

Making things

Steam from hot water can help make machines move, and cold water can cool down hot objects.

Making power

Water is used to make **hydro-electricity**.

Human effects on the water cycle

In the last 50 years, the human population has doubled, making the need for water even bigger. This is beginning to cause problems with the water cycle.

Dams

This is Claerwen **dam** in Wales. A dam can control a river flow and store water for uses such as hydro-electricity. This happens when the dam water flows into channels to make the water turbines turn. Turbines look like wheels with bucket-shaped blades around the edges. The water makes them move so fast that they can power generators to make electricity.

Dams can stop the rivers from flowing naturally, and cause run-off streams to **silt** up.

Large parts of the land are used to grow crops for food. Millions of litres of water are used for **irrigation**. This can cause water shortages and more problems for the water cycle.

Did you know?
....
70 per cent of the world's fresh water is used on crops.

Deforestation

Many of the world's forests are being cut down to use the land for building or to sell the wood. This is called deforestation.

Rainforests are especially in danger from deforestation.

Did you know?
Across the world, about 36 football fields worth of trees are cut down every minute.

Dangerous effects of deforestation

Not only is deforestation bad for the forest plants, but it also affects the water cycle for that area. Without the trees transpiring water into the air, the climate becomes drier, which makes the soil dry out. This can lead to **landslides** and **drought**. Fast surface run-off water which hasn't been slowed down by the trees and plants can cause sudden flooding, called **flash floods**.

a flash flood

Climate change

As the Earth's population gets bigger, the polluted fumes from factories and vehicles have started to change the Earth's weather patterns.

When pollution rises into the air, it can damage or make holes in Earth's protective outer layer, which is called the ozone layer.

Holes or thin parts of the ozone layer let in more heat from the sun, which causes the Earth's climate to get warmer.

Power stations and traffic pollute the Earth's atmosphere.

Melting icecaps

As the climate is getting warmer, the icecaps in the Arctic and Antarctica are beginning to melt. This means that there's more meltwater in the oceans to evaporate and condense into water droplets, creating higher rainfall all over the world.

Extreme weather

With the warming up of the Earth's climate, it's harder and harder to predict where rain precipitation will fall and how heavy it'll be. With more water in the air, heavy rain, storms and flooding have become more common.

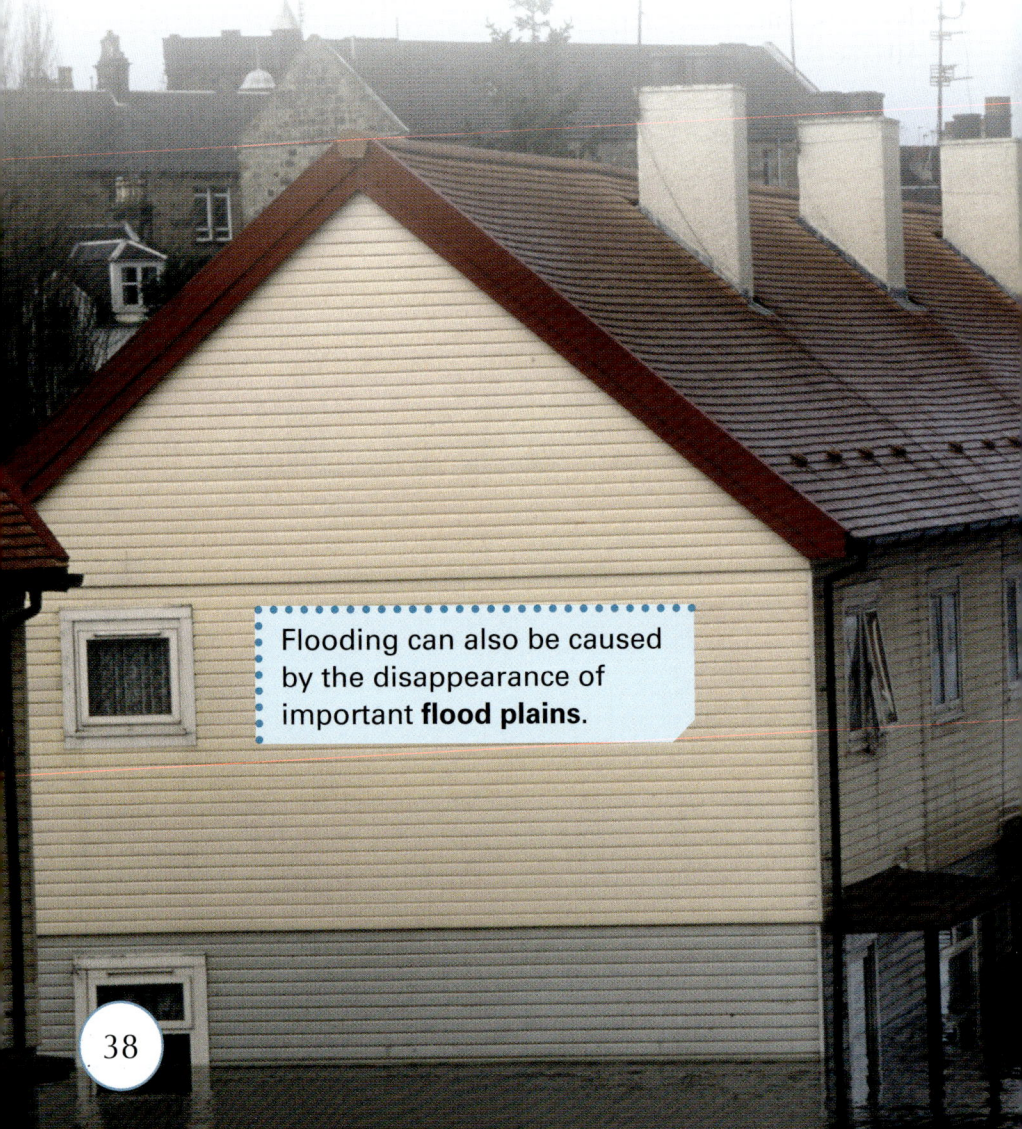

Flooding can also be caused by the disappearance of important **flood plains**.

SOMERSET VILLAGES FLOODED OUT

Non-stop heavy rain has flooded the villages in the Somerset Levels.

The villagers have had to quickly evacuate their flooded-out homes in small boats. The record rainfall is due to unusually high winds and heavy rainfall coming in from the Atlantic Ocean.

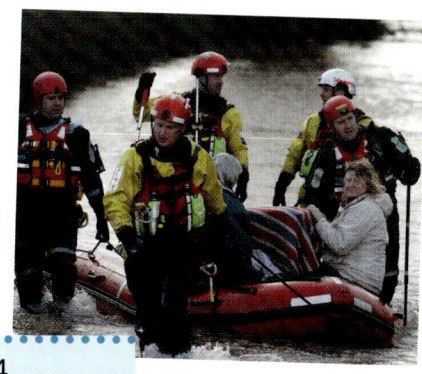

In 2013 and 2014, a flash flood happened in Somerset, UK.

39

The water footprint

If there's so much extra flood water, why are experts concerned about the planet's use of water? The main concern is making sure that fresh water is equally available to all of our planet's ever-growing population. Some countries and large industries use a lot more fresh water than they should, while others suffer from over-polluted water or lack of water due to drought.

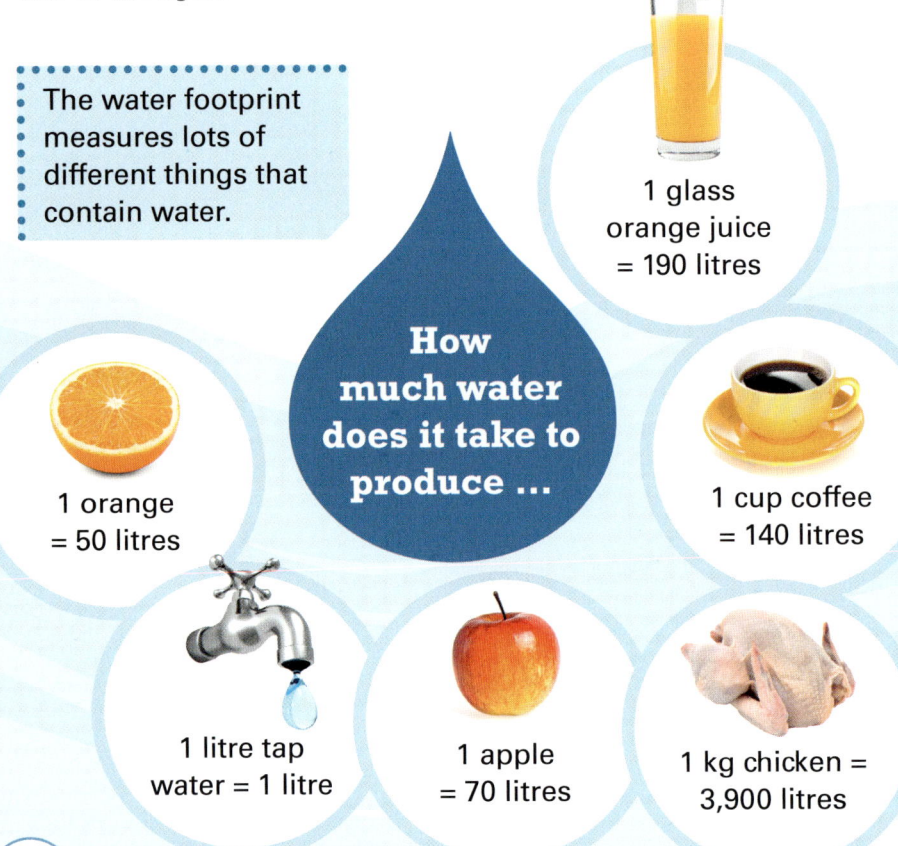

The water footprint measures lots of different things that contain water.

How much water does it take to produce ...

1 glass orange juice = 190 litres

1 orange = 50 litres

1 cup coffee = 140 litres

1 litre tap water = 1 litre

1 apple = 70 litres

1 kg chicken = 3,900 litres

Some experts are trying to sort out this imbalance with a plan called "the water footprint".

The water footprint helps people become more aware of how much fresh water they use and can save in their everyday life. It can be used to measure the water use of any group of people from one person, a class at school or the whole population of a country.

How big do you think your water footprint is?

1 glass apple juice = 190 litres

1 dozen eggs = 2,400 litres

1 litre bottled water = 5 litres

1 cup of tea = 30 litres

1 kg lamb = 4,800 litres

1 kg beef = 15,500 litres

1 kg soya beans = 1,800 litres

1 kg corn = 900 litres

1 kg wheat = 1,300 litres

Don't waste water!

The water footprint is a great way to cut down our water intake.

You can also save water by:

- drinking tap water, not bottled water

- turning off the water when it's not needed

- having a shower instead of a bath

- saving rainwater for watering plants.

Caring for the water cycle

Water is everywhere – in the air, underground, on the surface and in living things. It's constantly being recycled over and over again thanks to the amazing water cycle. However, it's in danger of becoming unbalanced due to human actions and climate change.

Without the water cycle, life on Earth couldn't survive, so it's up to us to make sure that we don't overuse water or damage the water cycle for future generations.

Glossary

bacteria — a group of tiny organisms that may carry disease

canal — man-made waterway to carry water to crops or for boats to travel inland

chlorine — a chemical used to kill bacteria in water

climates — types of weather often found in an area

dam — a large wall built across a river to control its flow or to use the water for other uses

drought — a long time without rain; a shortage of water

flash floods — fast and sudden floods due to heavy rain

flood plains — areas of land by a river that take water when it floods

fresh water — natural rainwater or ice that can be drunk

hydro-electricity — electricity power made from flowing water

irrigation — supplying water to the land and plants

landslides — areas of land or rock faces suddenly collapsing

reservoirs — man-made lakes to store water

silt — small materials in the water such as fine sand, grit and clay

vapour — an invisible type of gas

Index

aquifer 9, 29
clouds 2–4, 18–22
condensation 3, 16
dam 32
deforestation 34–35
drinking water 26–29
doppler radar 23
evaporation 3, 12–13
ground water 8–9, 14
flood 7, 10, 35, 38–40
humidity 25
hydro-electricity 31–32
irrigation 33
meltwater 7, 37
meteorologists 22

monsoon 21
ozone layer 36
precipitation 3–5, 38
radar 23
rainforest 24–25, 34
reservoir 26–27
run-off water 6–7, 14, 35
satellite 22
transpiration 3, 14–15, 25, 35
water cycle 2–4, 6, 14, 16, 18, 24–25, 32–33, 35, 43
water footprint 40–42
water vapour 12–13 16, 20, 25
weather forecasters 22, 23

45

Water world

precipitation

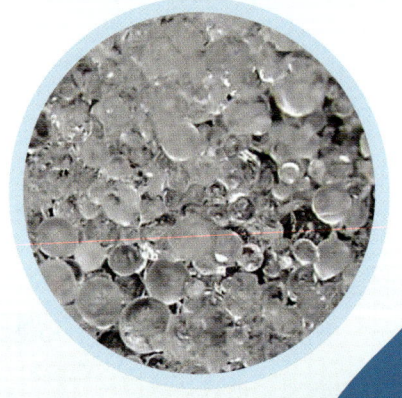

evaporation

transpiration

Where does water come from?

condensation

clouds

46

to make things

to drink

to help nature grow

to help crops grow

Why do we need water?

to make power

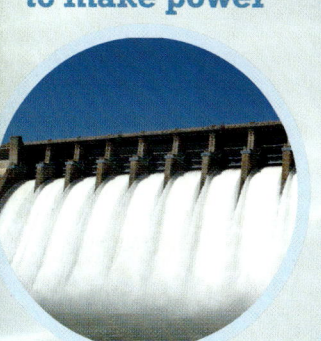

to put out fires

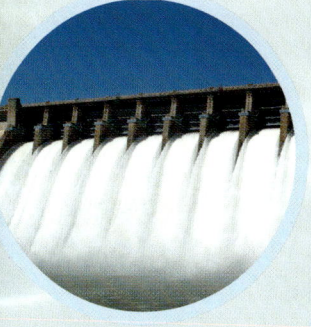

for fun

47

Ideas for reading

Written by Clare Dowdall, PhD
Lecturer and Primary Literacy Consultant

Reading objectives:
- retrieve and record information from non-fiction
- discuss their understanding and explain the meaning of words in context
- make predictions from details stated and applied

Spoken language objectives:
- give well-structured descriptions, explanations and narratives for different purposes

Curriculum links: Physical geography – the water cycle

Resources: containers for water, cloths, digital camera, paper and pencil

Build a context for reading
- Look at the front cover and discuss what is known about the water cycle. Collect known vocabulary that describes the stages, e.g. "evaporation".
- Check that children understand what a "cycle" is. Think of cycles that they are familiar with, e.g. life cycle.
- Read the blurb. Discuss what the word "recycle" means and what the prefix *re–* means, when applied to other words, e.g. "reopen".

Understand and apply reading strategies
- Read through the contents together helping children to decode challenging vocabulary, e.g. "precipitation", "evaporation", "transpiration" etc. Note the similar endings.
- Note any vocabulary that is unfamiliar on a whiteboard, and challenge children to find definitions through their reading.